Yoshio Sato

ANIMAL ORIGAMI

- **EASY TO MAKE**

- **FUN AND FANTASY**

- **PETS AND ZOO ANIMALS**

- **FEATURES THE NEW UNIT ORIGAMI METHOD**

KODANSHA USA

A Note from the Author

I have found origami to be a rewarding hobby for the young and old alike. Fashioning modest paper objects that can make people smile adds a certain relish to one's life. As I traveled to various countries to demonstrate my origami, I noticed that even if a common language did not exist between myself and those I taught or met by chance, we could communicate through origami. It gave these occasions a homespun pleasure and origami became a bridge between people in a simple yet profound way.

I hope that you will receive similar enjoyment from the origami animals in this small volume. Once you become proficient with the projects introduced in these pages, I urge you to go beyond the limitations of this book to create your own animals from the same basic units. The combinations are infinite.

A number of people ushered this book into being. Marge Wilson wrestled my basic text into pristine English. Kazuko Matsuzaki contributed vital spade work, checking and organizing the myriad details in the illustrations and captions. Akihiko Tokue's photographs captured the charm and effervescence of the origami. Natsumi Nakajima drew playful pastels to supplement the photography, then assembled all the pieces and added a delicate design touch all her own. And finally Michiko Uchiyama and Barry Lancet of Kodansha International provided overall guidance and vision, then checked and rechecked everything at every step along the way. My heartfelt gratitude goes out to one and all.

Published by Kodansha USA, Inc.
451 Park Avenue South, New York, NY 10016

Distributed in the United Kingdom and continental Europe by Kodansha Europe Ltd.

Copyright © 1996, 2013 by Yoshio Sato.
All rights reserved.
ISBN: 978-1-56836-505-3

First edition published in Japan in 1996 by Kodansha International
First US edition 2013 by Kodansha USA

Printed in Seoul, Korea, by Samhwa Printing Co, Ltd., arranged through Dai Nippon Printing Co., Ltd.
1st Printing, December 2012

www.kodanshausa.com

•• CONTENTS ••

General Information

About Origami and Origami Paper

"Origami," the Japanese word for paper folding, encompasses a challenging art form that stimulates creativity and imagination. With nothing more than a few sheets of paper, any adult or child can create charming, magical shapes.

In *Animal Origami*, rectangular paper is used rather than square origami sheets. Specifically, the paper measures about $3\frac{1}{2}$ by 5 inches (88 by 128 millimeters), but you can make it larger or smaller as you choose as long as the proportions remain the same (see the chart on the next page). At the back of this book there is enough colored stock to make 56 sheets of origami paper. Simply tear out a page of colored stock and cut in four. You can also use standard letter-size paper ($8\frac{1}{2}$ by 11 inches) or legal-size paper folded in fourths and cut. For best results, trim the quartered paper to the $3\frac{1}{2}$ by 5 inch size shown in the chart.

Before you use your best paper, you should practice with scratch paper. Cut newsprint or notebook paper to the required size, then go through the steps carefully. You will soon master them. When you're finished practicing, use the origami paper enclosed with this book or any other decorative paper, cut to the right proportion. Some papers you might consider to make more colorful animals include gift-wrap, old posters, craft paper, magazine pages, and wallpaper.

Enjoy your origami animals! There are endless possibilities for play. You could create a fantasy parade, zoo, or circus. You could use your animals to embellish a birthday gift for a friend, adorn a Christmas tree or other holiday items, or decorate your bedroom door. Try making a large version of your favorite animal and give it to a friend, with a special message written inside one of the folds. The number of uses for origami animals is unlimited, so use your imagination!

Level of Difficulty

The projects in *Animal Origami* are arranged in approximate order of difficulty, the easier folding projects at the front of the book, the more difficult ones toward the back. The origami fall into three basic categories:

Level A Beginning—easy to make.

Level B Intermediate—slight more challenging.

Level C Advanced—difficult in places.

In level A, all the steps for making the basic shapes are illustrated. In levels B and C, the instructions for making the basic unit shapes are abridged (but you can always refer to the unit chart on page 7). Try making one or two level A projects first. After you have mastered a few of them, move on to animals in levels B and C.

Suggestions

Making origami animals is simple and fun and provides hours of entertainment. With a few hours of practice you will be expert. Here are a few tips for making perfect origami:

1. Practice once or twice with scratch paper cut to size, then use colored paper.
2. Start with the colored-side face down so that it will become the outside of the completed origami. If your paper is colored on both sides, the color you wish to appear on the outside should be face down when you begin. *The outside surface is the shaded area throughout the instructions.*
3. Be sure to follow all instructions carefully and proceed in the sequence given. Do not skip or eliminate any steps.
4. The more exact your folds are, the more beautiful your finished work will be.
5. Follow any tips given in the text.

The shaded area below represents the "one full-size sheet of rectangular paper" used throughout this book. While there is enough colored stock in the back pages to make 56 full sheets of origami paper, if you wish to use different paper or make larger animals, use this chart as a guide for cutting new sheets.

To make larger sheets, align the bottom right corner of your sheet with the bottom right corner of this chart and lightly trace or copy the diagonal line onto your sheet of paper. The line should pass through the top left corner of any new paper size you make, as it does on the dotted sample in the chart. Make one sheet, then use it as a pattern to cut the rest of the sheets you need. To make even larger sheets, extend the line.

new paper size (sample)

full-size sheet
3 ½ by 5 inches
88 by 128 millimeters

"Unit Origami"

The system in this book relies on a series of simple units called "basic shapes." Each unit has a descriptive name such as "house," "boat," or "chair." The animals are built by combining two or more units. Sometimes the units are modified with additional folds to make more complex shapes, but the principles are always the same. The basic units are shown in the chart to the right. ➔

Folding Instructions

The key below shows all the folding instructions used in this book. For the most part, you will never need to refer to the key since the folding instructions are self-explanatory. But if you become confused, review the marks below before returning to the illustrated instructions.

LINES			
- - - - - - -	Indicates folds to be make in that step.	————	Indicates previous fold(s).
- · - · - · - · -	Indicates that paper should be folded behmd, or under.	· · · · · · · · · · · · · ·	Indicates (1) hidden portion or (2) position after fold.

SYMBOLS	
Fold forward along dotted line	Fold, then tuck in
Fold under along line	Fold the summit outward
Fold, then unfold	Fold forward, then back
Turn over	Rotate

6

BASIC SHAPES

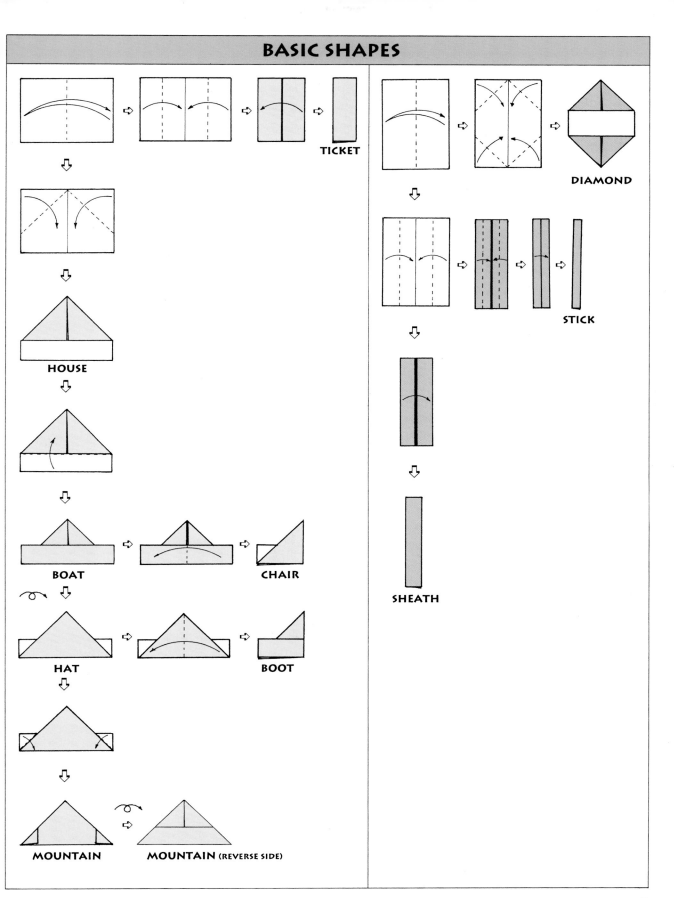

TICKET

DIAMOND

STICK

HOUSE

BOAT → CHAIR

SHEATH

HAT → BOOT

MOUNTAIN   MOUNTAIN (REVERSE SIDE)

CRAB

level A

Imagine a peaceful walk along the beach, waves crashing on the shore. Suddenly, a crab scurries across your path, its powerful legs and claws leaving their imprint in the wet sand. Watch your toes! For authenticity, use orange or tan colored paper.

MATERIALS
6 sheets of rectangular-shaped paper

MAKING THE BODY

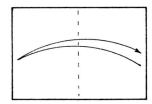

1. Fold a sheet of paper in half. Unfold.

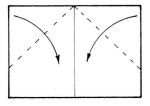

2. Fold the top corners down.

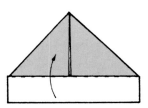

3. This is the HOUSE shape. Fold the bottom edge up.

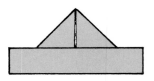

4. This is the BOAT shape.

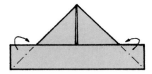

5. Fold both corners down and over the back to make a large triangle.

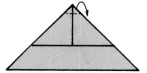

6. This is the reverse side of the MOUNTAIN shape. Fold top corner back. This is a modified MOUNTAIN shape.

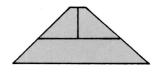

7. With a new sheet of paper make another modified MOUNTAIN shape.

MAKING THE CLAWS

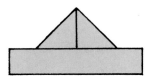

8. Fold as in steps 1 through 4 to make a BOAT shape.

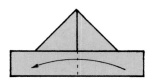

9. Fold in half.

10. This is the CHAIR shape. Make one more CHAIR shape for a second claw.

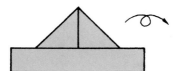

11. Fold as in steps 1 through 4 to make a BOAT shape. Turn over.

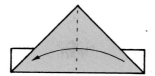

12. This is the HAT shape. Fold in half.

13. This is the BOOT shape. Make one more BOOT shape for the other leg.

CHECK!

Now you should have 6 pieces of folded paper.

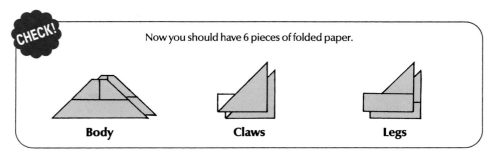

Body   **Claws**   **Legs**

●Let's put them together and make a Crab. This will require glue or paste to hold the shapes in place.●

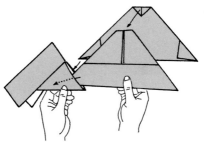

A. Glue or paste together the top small triangles of each modified MOUNTAIN shape to finish the body. Insert each of the two lower corners of the two body sections into each of the two slits in the leg as shown.

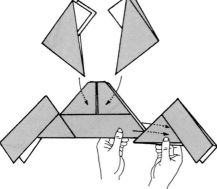

B. Attach the second leg the same way. Insert claws between the two body sections as shown, then glue or paste..

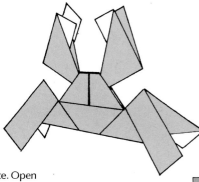

C. Your Crab is now complete. Open legs slightly to stand Crab up.

DOG
level A

Here's a pet dog that won't need to be trained, fed, or bathed. Reminiscent of the regal Airedale terrier, your dog is friendly, affectionate, and faithful. Use smaller sheets of paper to make puppies.

MATERIALS
3 sheets of rectangular-shaped paper
one 1/2 sheet paper for the head
one 1/4 sheet paper for the tail

MAKING THE CHEST & LEGS

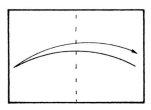

1. Fold a full-size sheet of paper in half. Unfold.

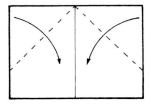

2. Fold down the top corners.

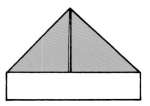

3. This is the HOUSE shape.

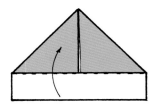

4. Fold bottom edge up.

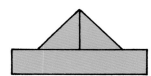

5. This is the BOAT shape. Repeat with a second sheet of paper to make same BOAT shape. These two BOAT shapes will form the chest and the front legs of the Dog.

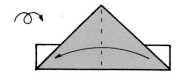

6. With a new sheet of paper, make another BOAT shape, then turn over and fold in half.

7. This BOOT shape will become the back legs of the Dog

MAKING THE HEAD

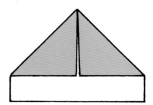

8. Fold the 1/2 sheet to make a HOUSE shape as in steps 1 and 2.

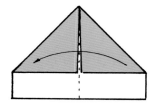

9. Fold in half.

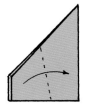

10. Fold the top layer back as shown.

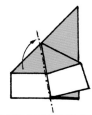

11. Fold the bottom layer under.

12. The head should look like this.

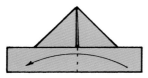

13. Fold the 1/4 sheet to make a BOAT shape as in steps 1 through 5. Fold in half.

14. This is the CHAIR shape for the tail of the Dog.

CHECK!

Now you should have 5 pieces of folded paper.

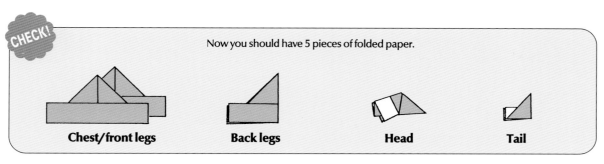

| **Chest/front legs** | **Back legs** | **Head** | **Tail** |

● Let's put them together and make a Dog. This will require glue or paste to hold the shapes in place. ●

A. Fold in the top corners of each BOAT shape as shown.

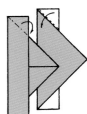

B. Fold top edges inward as shown to form ears. (Tip for beginners: Use a thin straight-edged ruler to help fold where the section tapers to a narrow margin.) Insert BOOT shape as shown between the two BOAT shapes to make legs. Hold all 3 shapes together in position as shown, then glue or paste in place.

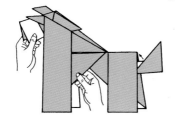

C. Insert face and tail as shown, then glue or paste. Tape the 2 BOAT shapes together at the top of the head behind the ears.

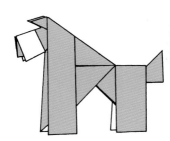

D. Your Dog is now complete. Open legs slightly to stand Dog up.

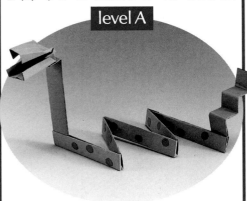

RATTLESNAKE
level A

The slithering snake has come to a sudden stop. He is poised to strike, his rattles vibrating loudly. You will usually hear the hissing and rattling sound before you ever see him. Be careful . . . he is dangerous! You can make fangs by folding and crimping the corners of the top flaps on the inside of the snake's mouth.

MATERIALS
8 sheets of rectangular-shaped paper

MAKING THE BODY & RATTLE

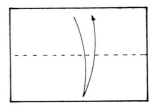

1. Fold a sheet of paper in half. Unfold.

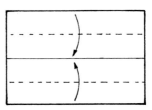

2. Fold both edges to the center.

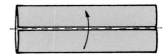

3. Fold in half.

4. This is the SHEATH shape and it will become part of the Snake's body. Repeat steps 1 through 4 to make six more SHEATH shapes.

5. You now have seven SHEATH shapes. Set one aside. On three of them, fold the right edge as shown. On two of them, fold the left edge in. These will become the body of the snake.

6. Fold the last SHEATH five times as shown. This will become the rattle.

MAKING THE HEAD

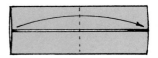

7. Repeat steps 1 and 2, then fold in half as shown.

8. Fold the left-hand corners. Unfold.

9. Tuck in the corners.

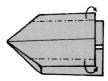

10. Fold both edges of the top layer inside as shown. (See next illustration.)

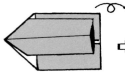 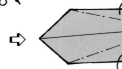

11. Turn over and fold both edges inside.

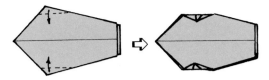
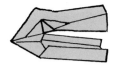

12. Fold the top and bottom corners of the top layer as shown. Make eyes by unfolding 90° so that the triangular portion stands straight up.

13. This will become the head of the Snake.

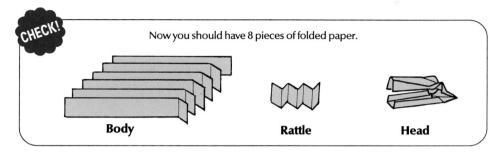

CHECK!

Now you should have 8 pieces of folded paper.

Body　　　**Rattle**　　　**Head**

●Let's put them together and make a Rattlesnake. This will require glue or paste to hold the shapes in place.●

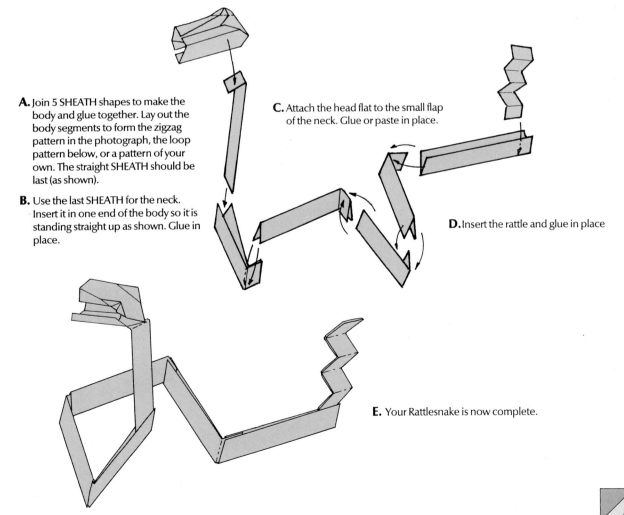

A. Join 5 SHEATH shapes to make the body and glue together. Lay out the body segments to form the zigzag pattern in the photograph, the loop pattern below, or a pattern of your own. The straight SHEATH should be last (as shown).

B. Use the last SHEATH for the neck. Insert it in one end of the body so it is standing straight up as shown. Glue in place.

C. Attach the head flat to the small flap of the neck. Glue or paste in place.

D. Insert the rattle and glue in place

E. Your Rattlesnake is now complete.

MOUSE
level A

The mouse is a small, simple, peace-loving creature. Having scampered across the floor, it stops suddenly on its haunches, listening intently. No enemy appears to be near. Time to safely nibble! For a more realistic look, round off the top of the ears with a scissors and consider drawing on eyes or cutting thin strips of paper to make whiskers.

MATERIALS
4 sheets of rectangular-shaped paper

MAKING THE BODY

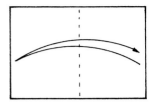

1. Fold a sheet of paper in half. Unfold.

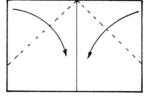

2. Fold down the top corners.

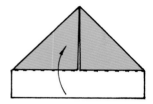

3. Fold the bottom edge up.

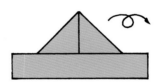

4. This is the BOAT shape. Turn over.

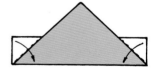

5. Fold both corners down to make a large triangle.

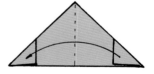

6. This is the MOUNTAIN shape. Fold in half.

7. This is a modified MOUNTAIN shape. With a new sheet of paper, make a new modified MOUNTAIN shape.

MAKING THE HEAD

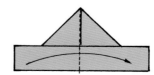

8. Fold one sheet of paper as in steps 1 through 4 to make the BOAT shape. Fold in half.

9. This is the CHAIR shape. Tuck in the top corner and fold the front flap up as shown. Fold the rear flap back in the same manner.

10. This will be the head of the Mouse.

14

MAKING THE TAIL

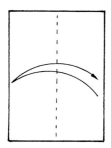

11. Fold a sheet of paper in half. Unfold.

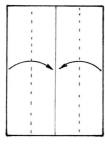

12. Fold both sides into the center as shown.

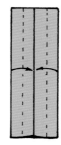

13. Fold both sides again into the center as shown.

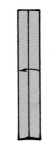

14. Fold in half.

15. This STICK shape will be the tail of the Mouse.

CHECK! Now you should have 4 pieces of folded paper.

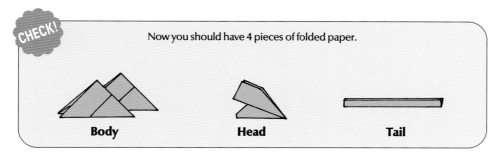

Body   **Head**   **Tail**

● Let's put them together and make a Mouse. This will require glue or paste to hold the shapes in place. ●

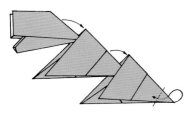

A. Insert the head into one section of the body as shown, then insert into the second body section. Glue or paste in place. Fold the bottom corner of the body, then tuck in as shown.

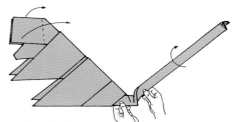

B. Fold each flap of the head as shown to make ears. Insert tail, then glue and twist.

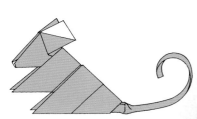

C. Roll the tail up around a pencil or thin stick to make it curl. Your Mouse is now complete.

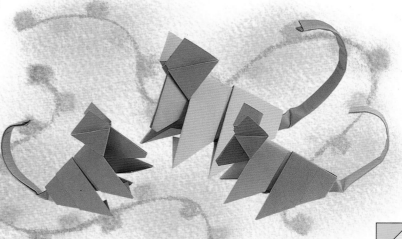

RABBITS

level A

Rabbits love to munch and gnaw on fresh, crispy vegetables. Their long ears must listen constantly for danger. At a moment's notice, they must be ready to hop or run quickly to safety. Use gray or brown paper to make your rabbit look more realistic. Use smaller pieces of paper to create baby bunnies. If you want a cottontail rabbit, paste a cottonball where the tail should be.

MATERIALS (for Sitting Rabbit)
3 sheets of rectangular-shaped paper

MATERIALS (for Running Rabbit)
4 sheets of rectangular-shaped paper

SITTING RABBIT
MAKING THE HEAD

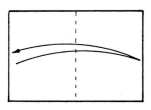

1. Fold one sheet of paper in half. Unfold.

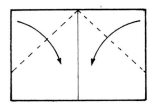

2. Fold down the top corners.

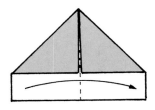

3. This is the HOUSE shape. Fold in half.

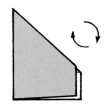

4. Rotate clockwise as shown.

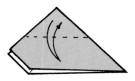

5. Fold down the top corner. Unfold.

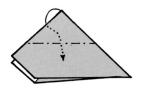

6. Fold triangle area inward.

7. Fold the left flap on the top layer up.

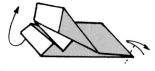

8. Do the same for the bottom layer. Fold the right tiny corner as shown. Unfold.

9. Fold the tiny right corner inward. Fold the bottom triangle part formed by the last fold. Unfold.

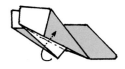

10. Fold the bottom triangle area inward.

11. This will be the head of the Rabbit.

MAKING THE BODY

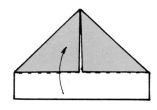

12. Fold a sheet of paper as in steps 1 and 2 to make the HOUSE shape. Fold the bottom edge up.

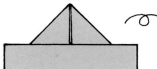

13. This is the BOAT shape. Turn over.

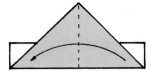

14. This is the HAT shape. Fold in half.

15. This is the BOOT shape. Make one more BOOT shape.

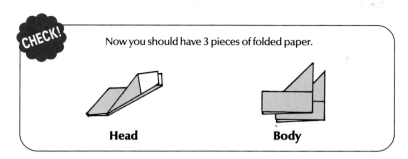

CHECK! Now you should have 3 pieces of folded paper.

Head

Body

●Let's put them together and make a Sitting Rabbit. This will require glue or paste to hold the shapes in place.●

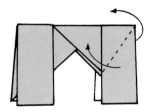

A. Insert one BOOT shape into the other as shown. Glue or paste in place. Fold the right flap on the top layer up as shown to make a rear leg. Do the same for the bottom layer.

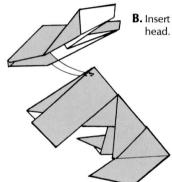

B. Insert the body into the slit in the head. Glue or paste in place.

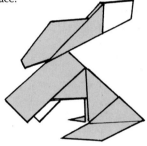

C. Your Sitting Rabbit is now complete.

RUNNING RABBIT

MAKING THE HEAD

1. Make the same head as for the Sitting Rabbit

MAKING THE BODY & LEGS

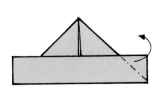

2. Make two BOAT shapes as in steps 12 and 13. Fold the right flap back on one BOAT shape and fold the left flap back on the second BOAT.

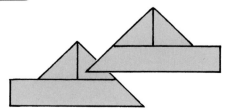

3. These will become the front legs and body of the Running Rabbit.

4. Fold a sheet of paper as in steps 12 to 15 of the Sitting Rabbit to make a BOOT shape. This will become the back legs.

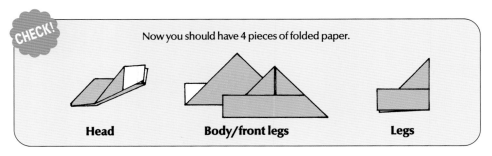

Now you should have 4 pieces of folded paper.

Head   **Body/front legs**   **Legs**

●Let's put them together and make a Running Rabbit. This will require glue or paste to hold the shapes in place.●

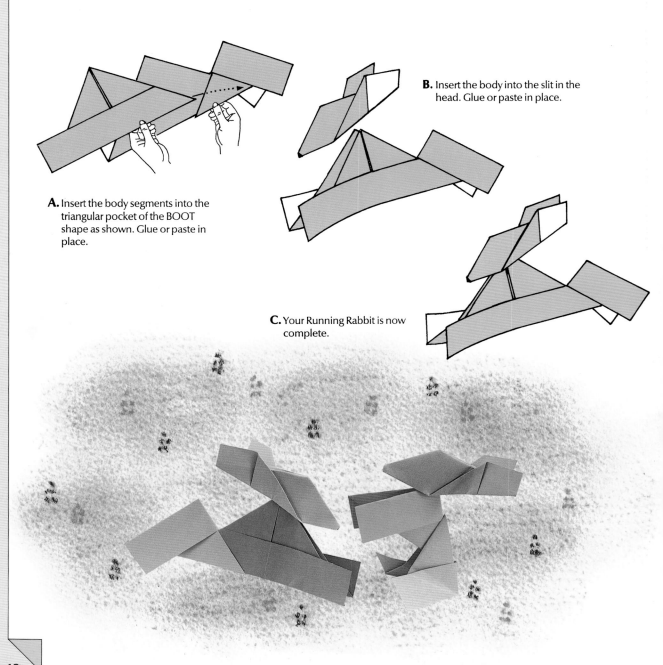

A. Insert the body segments into the triangular pocket of the BOOT shape as shown. Glue or paste in place.

B. Insert the body into the slit in the head. Glue or paste in place.

C. Your Running Rabbit is now complete.

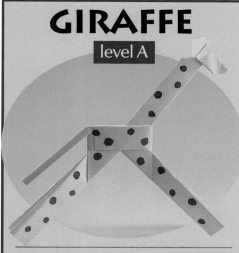

GIRAFFE

level A

The giraffe uses his long legs and neck to help him reach leaves in the treetops. Use a thicker paper so the giraffe will be able to stand on its long legs. You can add a "tuft" to the end of the tail. Make it from a light-weight yarn or thin strips of paper. You can also create a mane for the giraffe with the same material.

MATERIALS
7 sheets of rectangular-shaped paper
one 1/2 sheet paper for the head
one 1/2 sheet paper for the tail

MAKING THE BODY

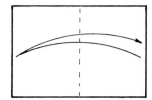

1. Fold a full-size sheet of paper in half. Unfold.

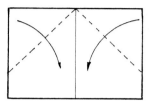

2. Fold down the top corners.

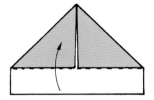

3. Fold the bottom edge up.

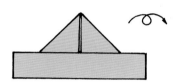

4. This is the BOAT shape. Turn over.

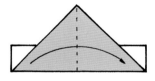

5. This is the HAT shape. Fold in half.

6. This is the BOOT shape. With another sheet of paper, make one more BOOT shape.

MAKING THE LEGS

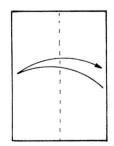

7. Fold paper in half. Unfold.

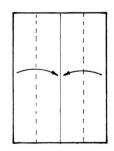

8. Fold both sides to the center.

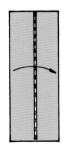

9. Fold in half.

10. This is the SHEATH shape. Make three more SHEATH shapes.

19

MAKING THE NECK

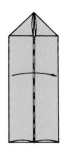

11. Fold a sheet of paper as in steps 7 through 9. Unfold as shown. Fold down the top corners.

12. Fold in half.

13. This is a modified SHEATH shape for the neck of the Giraffe.

MAKING THE HEAD

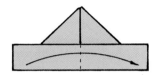

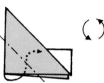

14. Fold a 1/2 sheet of paper as in steps 1 through 4 to make the BOAT shape. Fold in half.

15. This is the CHAIR shape. Fold the left corner up, then unfold.

16. Fold and tuck in corner. Rotate 90° counterclockwise.

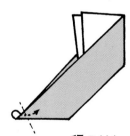

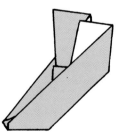

17. Fold the pointed end in.

18. This is the head of the Giraffe.

MAKING THE TAIL

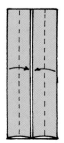

19. Fold a 1/2 sheet of paper as in steps 7 and 8. Fold both sides to the center again.

21. This STICK shape will be the tail of the Giraffe.

20. Fold in half.

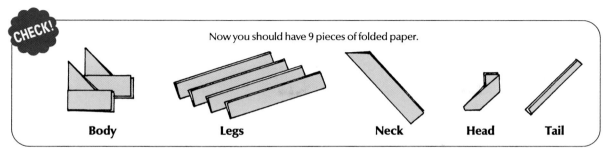

Now you should have 9 pieces of folded paper.

Body   **Legs**   **Neck**   **Head**   **Tail**

●Let's put them together and make a Giraffe. This will require glue or paste to hold the shapes in place.●

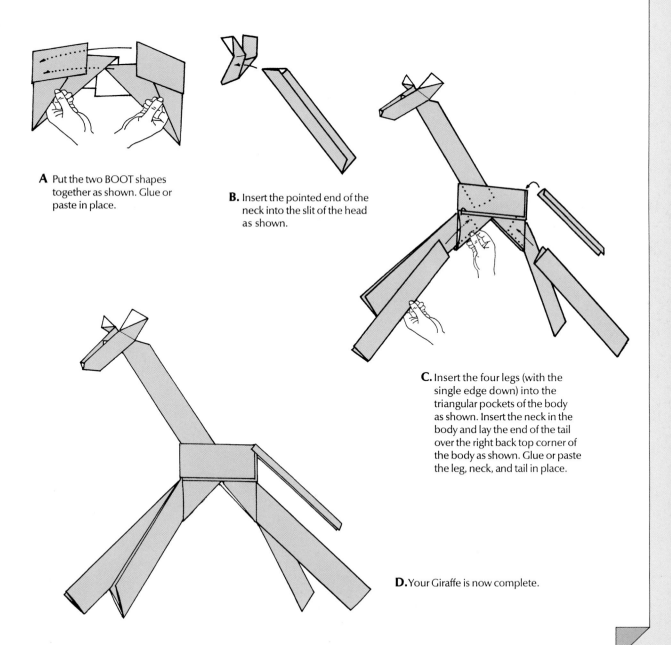

A Put the two BOOT shapes together as shown. Glue or paste in place.

B. Insert the pointed end of the neck into the slit of the head as shown.

C. Insert the four legs (with the single edge down) into the triangular pockets of the body as shown. Insert the neck in the body and lay the end of the tail over the right back top corner of the body as shown. Glue or paste the leg, neck, and tail in place.

D. Your Giraffe is now complete.

BIRDS

These small feathered friends could be pigeons, sparrows, or doves. The Standing Bird might be perched on a tree branch, singing a song. The Landing Bird could be swooping down to snatch up a tasty grain, fruit, or insect. Or perhaps it's simply returning to its nest. The Flying Bird, soaring peacefully through a clear blue sky, must be the happiest bird of them all!

MATERIALS (for Standing Bird)
2 sheets of rectangular-shaped paper
one 1/2 sheet of paper for the legs

MATERIALS (for Flying Bird)
2 sheets of rectangular-shaped paper
two 1/2 sheets of paper for the wings

MATERIALS (for Landing Bird)
2 sheets of rectangular-shaped paper
three 1/2 sheets of paper for
the legs and the wings

STANDING BIRD
MAKING THE BODY

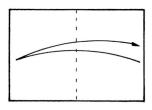

1. Fold a full-size sheet of paper in half. Unfold.

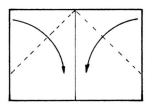

2. Fold down the top corners.

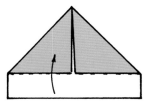

3. This is the HOUSE shape. Fold bottom edge up.

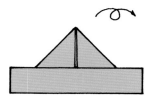

4. Turn over.

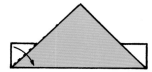

5. This is the HAT shape. Fold the left flap down.

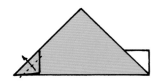

6. Fold back as shown.

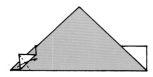

7. Fold the tiny bottom corner up.

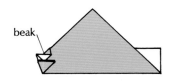

beak

8. This modified HAT shape will become the side of the bird's body **with the beak**.

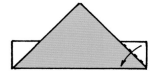

9. With another full-size sheet of paper, repeat steps 1 through 4 to make another HAT shape, then fold the right flap down.

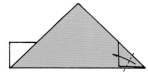

10. Fold the right bottom corner up.

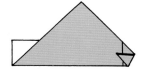

11. This modified HAT shape will become the other side of the bird's body **without** the beak.

MAKING THE LEGS

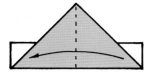

12. With a half-size sheet of paper, repeat steps 1 through 4 to make the HAT shape. Fold in half.

13. This is the BOOT shape. Fold the right bottom corner up. Unfold.

14. Tuck in the triangular section.

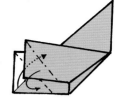

15. Fold the back and front flaps in as shown.

CHECK!

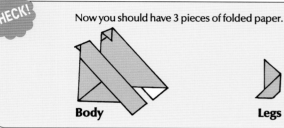

Now you should have 3 pieces of folded paper.

Body **Legs**

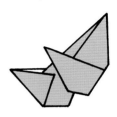

16. This is a modified BOOT shape and will be the legs of the Bird.

● Let's put them together and make a Standing Bird.
This will require glue or paste to hold the shapes in place. ●

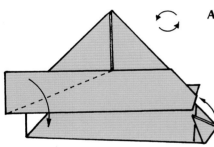

A. Put the two modified HAT shapes together and put glue on the interior bottom edge and small triangle at the right. Fold the left flap down and do the same for the reverse side. Rotate counterclockwise until beak is upright.

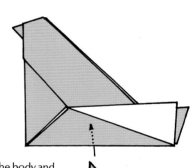

B. Insert the legs into the body and paste or glue. Adjust the legs as necessary to keep the bird balanced.

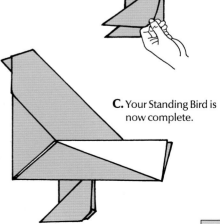

C. Your Standing Bird is now complete.

FLYING BIRD

MAKING THE BODY

1. Repeat steps 1 to 11 for the Standing Bird to make the body.

MAKING THE WINGS

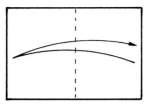

2. Fold a 1/2 sheet of paper in half. Unfold.

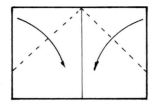

3. Fold down the top corners.

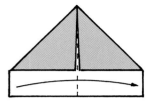

4. This is the HOUSE shape. Fold in half.

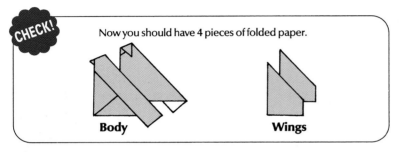

CHECK! Now you should have 4 pieces of folded paper.

Body

Wings

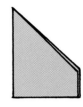

5. This will be one wing. Repeat steps 2 to 4 to make a second wing.

● **Let's put them together and make a Flying Bird.**
This will require glue or paste to hold the shapes in place. ●

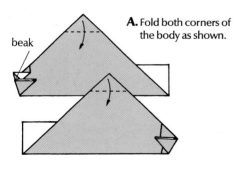

A. Fold both corners of the body as shown.

beak

B. Place the triangle with the beak over the other triangle. Put glue on the interior bottom edge and the small triangle at the right. Fold the left flap down and do the same for the reverse side.

beak

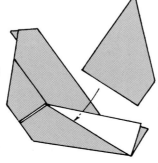

C. Rotate as shown. Insert each wing between the body and triangle flap. Paste or glue in place.

D. Your Flying Bird is now complete.

LANDING BIRD
MAKING THE BODY, LEGS & WINGS

1. Repeat steps 1 through 16 for the Standing Bird to make the body and legs.

2. Repeat steps 2 through 5 for the Flying Bird to make the wings.

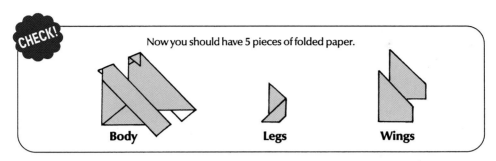

CHECK!

Now you should have 5 pieces of folded paper.

Body   **Legs**   **Wings**

● Let's put them together and make a Landing Bird. This will require glue or paste to hold the shapes in place. ●

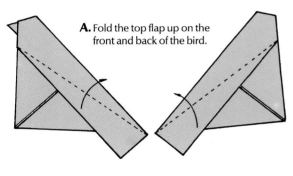

A. Fold the top flap up on the front and back of the bird.

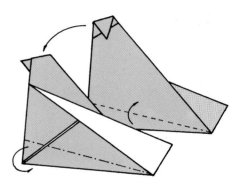

B. Fold the bottom flap under as shown. Repeat with back section. Paste the two body parts together.

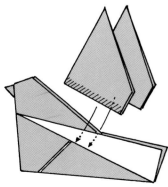

C. Insert each wing between the body and the triangular flap. Glue along the bottom outside edge of both wings (shaded area).

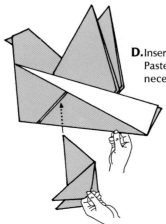

D. Insert the legs into the body Paste or glue. Open legs as necessary after glue dries.

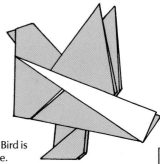

E. Your Landing Bird is now complete.

25

PIG

level A

Squealing with delight, your pig rolls in the mud, then waddles toward you flapping his ears. Hear him oink, snort, and grunt. He will look even more realistic if you use pink or orange paper.

MATERIALS
4 sheets of rectangular-shaped paper
one 1/4 sheet of paper for the tail

MAKING THE BODY & LEGS

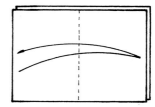

1. Use two full-size sheets of paper and fold in half. Unfold.

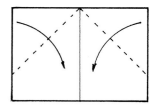

2. Fold down the top corners.

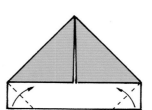

3. This is the HOUSE shape. Fold both bottom corners up.

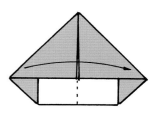

4. Fold in half. This will be the hips and back legs of the Pig.

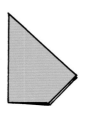

5. With one full-size sheet of paper, repeat steps 1 through 4 to make the breast and front legs.

MAKING THE HEAD

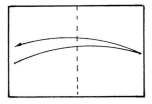

6. Fold a full-size sheet of paper in half. Unfold.

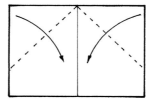

7. Fold the top corners down.

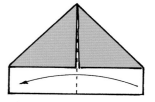

8. This is the HOUSE shape. Fold in half.

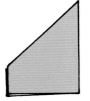

9. Rotate 45° clockwise. Fold the bottom corner up. Unfold.

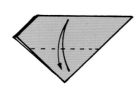

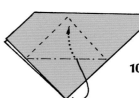

10. Tuck in the lower triangle to the top edge.

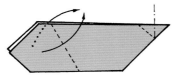

11. Fold the left flap on the top layer up. Repeat on the reverse side. Make two folds on the right-hand corner, then unfold.

12. Make the nose by opening up the right corner and then collapsing as shown. This is the head of the Pig.

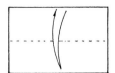

13. Fold a 1/4 sheet of paper in half. Unfold.

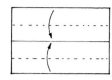

14. Fold both sides into the center as shown.

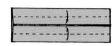

15. Fold both sides in again.

16. Fold in half.

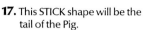

17. This STICK shape will be the tail of the Pig.

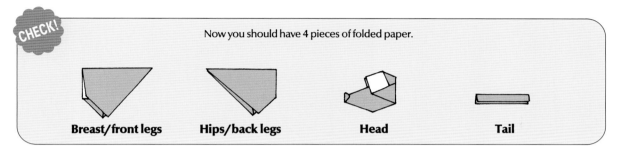

Now you should have 4 pieces of folded paper.

Breast/front legs **Hips/back legs** **Head** **Tail**

●Let's put them together and make a Pig. This will require glue or paste to hold the shapes in place.●

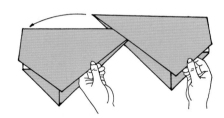

A. Place the hips/back legs (doubled paper) over the breast and front legs as shown. Glue or paste in place.

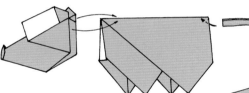

B. Insert the body into the folded crease in the back of the head. Twist the tail to curl it, and insert between the back legs of the Pig as shown. Glue or paste in place. Spread legs slightly.

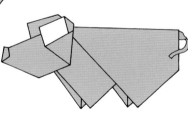

C. Your Pig is now complete.

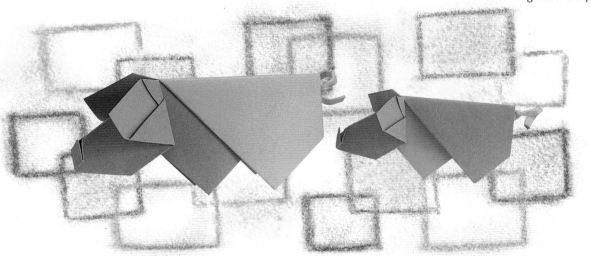

ELEPHANT

level A

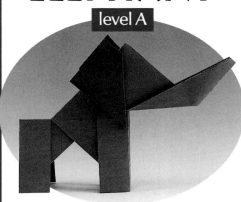

Although the elephant is the largest and most powerful of all living land mammals, it is gentle and peaceful. A throaty rumbling sound means your elephant is talking. You can also flap its ears. Elephants are an endangered species, so take good care of him! Use gray or brown paper for authenticity.

MATERIALS
4 sheets of rectangular-shaped paper
two 1/2 sheets of paper for the ears

MAKING THE CHEST & LEGS

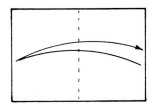

1. Fold a full-size sheet of paper in half. Unfold.

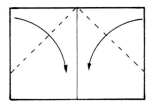

2. Fold down the top corners.

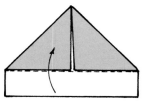

3. Fold bottom edge up.

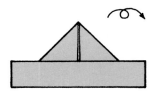

4. This is the HAT shape. Make a second HAT shape. Turn over.

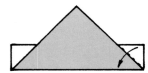 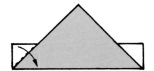

5. Fold the right corner down on one HAT, the left corner down on the other hat.

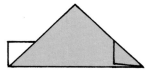 

6. These modified HAT shapes will become the chest and front legs of the Elephant.

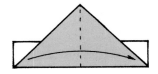

7. Make one more HAT shape as in steps 1 through 4. Fold in half.

8. This BOOT shape will be the hips and back legs of the Elephant.

MAKING THE HEAD & TRUNK

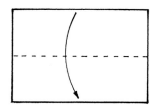

9. Fold a full-size paper in half.

10. Fold the left corner of the top layer up as shown. Fold the bottom layer back in the same manner.

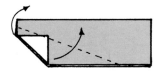

11. Fold the top layer up as shown. Fold the bottom layer back.

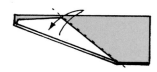

12. Fold as shown. Unfold.

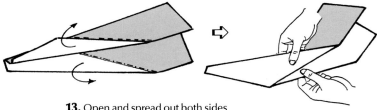

13. Open and spread out both sides as shown and make the shape.

14. The head and trunk should look like this.

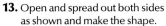

MAKING THE EARS

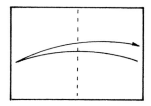

15. Fold a 1/2 sheet of paper in half. Unfold.

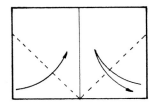

16. Fold the left bottom corner up. Fold the right corner up, then unfold.

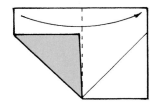

17. Fold in half.

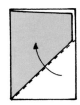

18. Fold the right corner up.

19. This is the left ear.

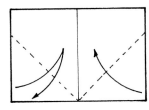 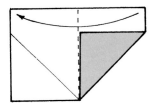 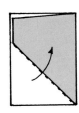 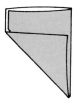

20. To make the right ear, fold another 1/2 sheet of paper as shown.

CHECK!

Now you should have 6 pieces of folded paper.

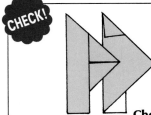 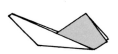

Chest / front legs   **Back legs**   **Head /trunk**   **Ears**

● Let's put them together and make an Elephant. This will require glue or paste to hold the shapes in place. ●

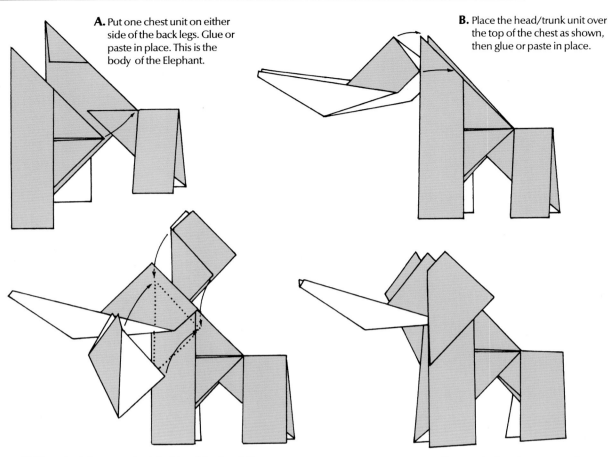

A. Put one chest unit on either side of the back legs. Glue or paste in place. This is the body of the Elephant.

B. Place the head/trunk unit over the top of the chest as shown, then glue or paste in place.

C. Place the left ear on the left side of the head. Tape or paste the smaller flap (the corner that forms a triangle) to the trunk and body assembly. Glue the right ear on the other side of the head. (The base of the triangle should be parallel to the front legs.)

D. Your Elephant is now complete.

LION
level B

The lion stands majestic and powerful, surveying his territory. His long mane blows in the hot, dry wind. The king of beasts is feared and respected. In the evening, his famous roar announces his intention to begin the night's hunt. For authenticity, you could use yellow or light brown for the body, and darker for the mane and tail.

MATERIALS
8 sheets of rectangular-shaped paper

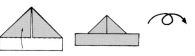

1. Make the HAT shape. Fold the right corner over the front.

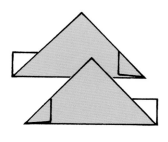

2. This is a modified HAT shape. With another sheet of paper, make another HAT shape but this time fold the left corner over. These modified HAT shapes will become the chest and front legs.

3. Make the BOOT shape. This will become the back legs of the Lion.

4. Make the TICKET shape for the belly of the Lion.

31

MAKING THE HEAD

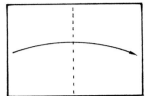

5. Fold a sheet of paper in half.

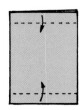

6. Fold in the top and bottom edges.

7. Fold in half.

8. Make the two folds on the left top corner as shown.

 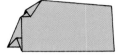

9. Flatten the left top corner as shown. Place your finger in the slit and spread the bottom outward as shown.

MAKING THE MANE

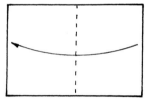

10. Fold a sheet of paper in half.

11. Fold the left corner up.

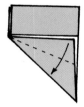

12. Fold the top layer to the left as shown.

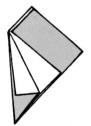 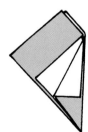

13. This is the shape for the left side of the mane. With another sheet of paper, fold as in steps 10 through 12. (In step 11, you must fold the right corner up, then fold the top flap back to make the right side of the mane.)

MAKING THE TAIL

14. Make the STICK shape. Fold both sides as shown. Unfold.

15. Open the STICK shape. Fold both ends as shown. This modified STICK shape will be the tail.

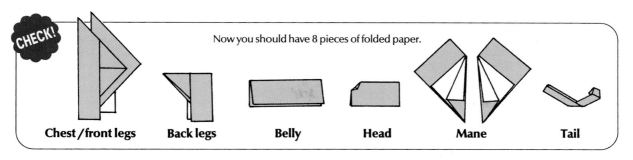

Now you should have 8 pieces of folded paper.

Chest /front legs **Back legs** **Belly** **Head** **Mane** **Tail**

●Let's put them together and make a Lion. This will require glue or paste to hold the shapes in place.●

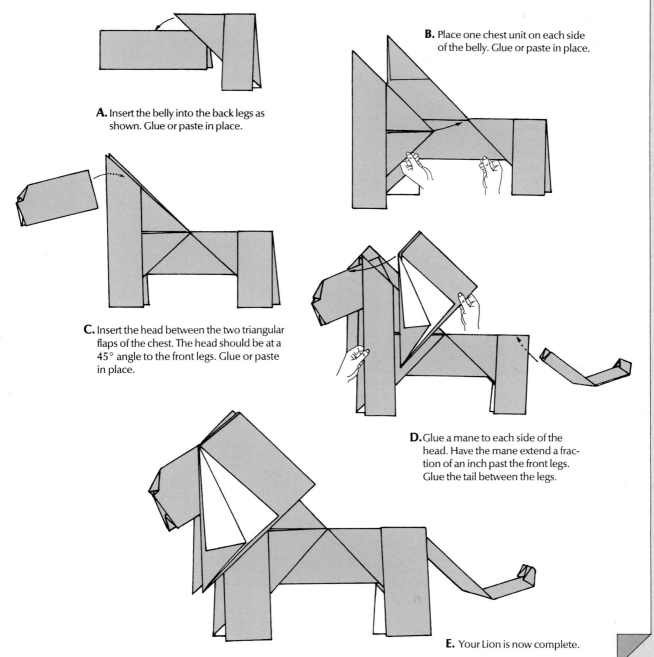

A. Insert the belly into the back legs as shown. Glue or paste in place.

B. Place one chest unit on each side of the belly. Glue or paste in place.

C. Insert the head between the two triangular flaps of the chest. The head should be at a 45° angle to the front legs. Glue or paste in place.

D. Glue a mane to each side of the head. Have the mane extend a fraction of an inch past the front legs. Glue the tail between the legs.

E. Your Lion is now complete.

KANGAROO
level B

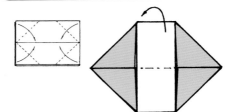

MAKING THE BODY

1. Use two full-size sheets of paper and fold in corners to make the DIAMOND shape. Fold the top half back.

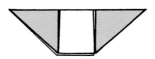

2. The body of the Kangaroo should look like this.

Kangaroos have powerful hind legs for jumping and a long tail which helps it balance. Try folding a smaller version to make a baby kangaroo. You can let it snuggle in its mother's pouch.

MATERIALS
5 sheets of rectangular-shaped paper
one 1/2 sheet of paper for the head

MAKING THE FRONT LEGS

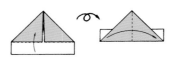

3. With a full-size sheet of paper, make the BOOT shape for the front legs.

MAKING THE BACK LEGS

4. With a full-size sheet of paper, make the BOOT shape. Fold the left bottom corner as shown. Unfold.

5. Tuck the bottom triangle inside as shown.

6. The back legs of the Kangaroo should look like this.

MAKING THE TAIL

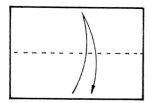

7. Fold a full-size sheet of paper in half. Unfold.

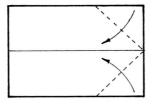

8. Fold the right corners to the center.

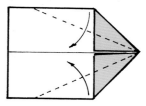

9. Fold both corners to the center again.

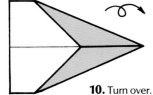

10. Turn over.

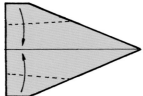

11. Fold the top and bottom edges as shown.

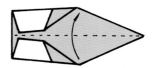

12. Fold in half.

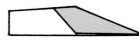

13. The tail should look like this.

MAKING THE HEAD

 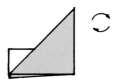

14. Using a 1/2 size sheet of paper, make the CHAIR shape. Rotate 90°.

15. Fold the left bottom corner as shown. Unfold.

16. Tuck in the corners.

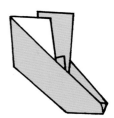

17. This will be the head of the Kangaroo.

Now you should have 5 pieces of folded paper.

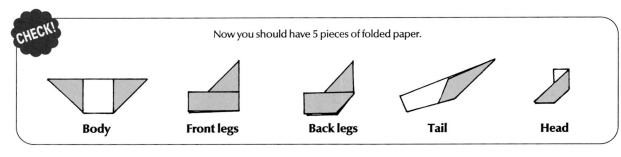

| Body | Front legs | Back legs | Tail | Head |

●Let's put them together and make a Kangaroo. This will require glue or paste to hold the shapes in place.●

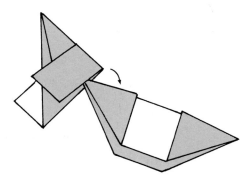

A. Insert the left edge of the body into the front legs as shown. Glue or paste in place.

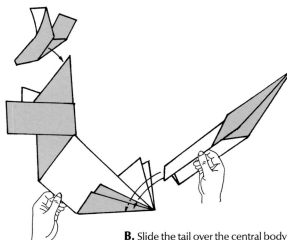

B. Slide the tail over the central body fold. Glue or paste. Place the head over the sharp corner above the front legs. Glue or paste.

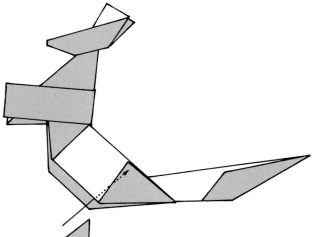

C. Insert the back legs into the body as shown. After the glue has dried, open the legs to balance the Kangaroo.

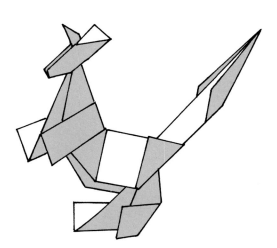

D. Your Kangaroo is now complete.

ROOSTER

level B

The strongest rooster rules the chicken coop. Early morning brings his daily wake-up call. Your rooster is ready to crow. Cock-a-doodle-do! You can paint his comb and beak red to make him more lifelike.

MATERIALS
7 sheets of rectangular-shaped paper
one 1/2 sheet of paper for the head

MAKING THE BODY

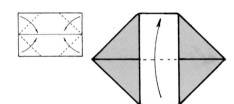

1. With two sheets of full-size paper, make the DIAMOND shape. Fold in half.

2. The body of the Rooster should look like this.

MAKING THE LEGS

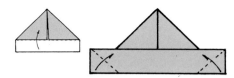

3. With a full-size sheet of paper, make the BOAT shape. Fold bottom corners up.

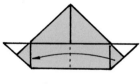

4. Fold in half.

5. This modified BOAT shape will be the legs for the Rooster.

MAKING THE BREAST

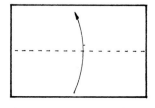

6. Fold a full-size sheet of paper in half. Be sure that the top side is open.

7. Fold both bottom corners up. Unfold.

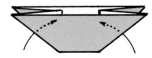

8. Tuck both bottom triangle parts in as shown.

MAKING THE TAIL

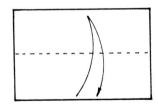

9. Fold a full-size sheet of paper in half. Unfold.

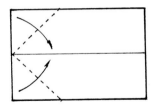

10. Fold both left corners to the center.

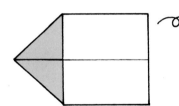

11. Turn over.

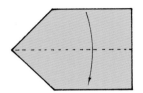

12. Fold in half.

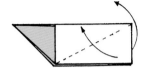

13. Fold the top layer up. Do the same for the bottom layer.

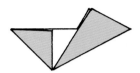

14. The tail of the Rooster should look like this.

MAKING THE WINGS

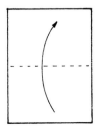

15. Fold a full-size sheet of paper in half.

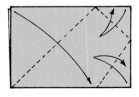

16. Fold down the left top corner. Fold both right corners and unfold.

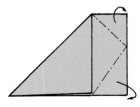

17. Fold both right corners backward.

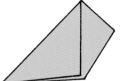

18. Turn over. This is the right wing.

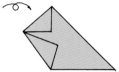

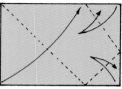

19. With another full-size sheet of paper, make the left wing by following 15 through 17, but fold along the lines in the diagram above.

MAKING THE HEAD

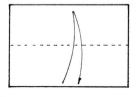

20. Fold a 1/2 size sheet of paper in half. Unfold.

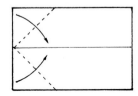

21. Fold both left corners to the center.

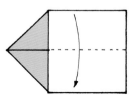

22. Fold in half.

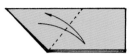

23. Fold the left triangle part down. Unfold. Rotate 90° clockwise.

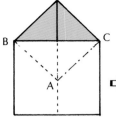
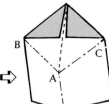

24. Unfold and push up from underneath at point A until lines AB and AC pop up, then bring points B and C together.

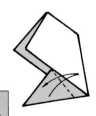

25. Fold the bottom triangle part as shown. Unfold.

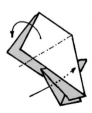

26. Tuck in the triangle part and fold the top flap back. Turn over.

27. This will be the head of the Rooster.

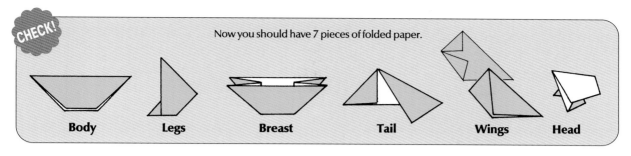

CHECK!

Now you should have 7 pieces of folded paper.

Body **Legs** **Breast** **Tail** **Wings** **Head**

●Let's put them together and make a Rooster. This will require glue or paste to hold the shapes in place.●

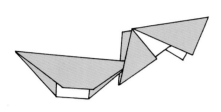

A. Insert the body into the tail as shown. Glue or paste in place.

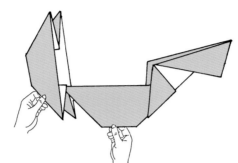

B. Insert the other corner of the body into the breast, then paste.

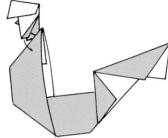

C. Set the head on the breast. Glue in place.

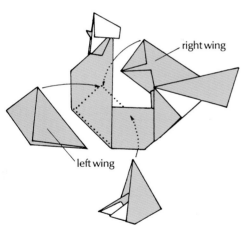

right wing

left wing

D. Attach each wing to its side of the breast as shown and glue. Insert the legs in the body, then glue. When glue has dried, adjust the legs slightly for stability if necessary.

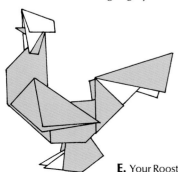

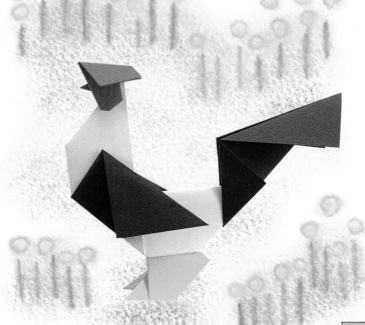

E. Your Rooster is now complete.

PENGUIN

level C

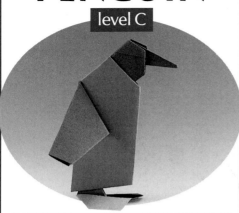

The penguin is a flightless marine bird. It is well adapted to the water and extreme cold. Known for its clumsy waddling style of walking on land, the penguin actually moves gracefully and quickly in water. To make your penguin more like the real thing, color his back dark and make his belly white.

MATERIALS
2 sheets of rectangular-shaped paper
two 1/2 sheets of paper for the head and legs

MAKING THE BODY

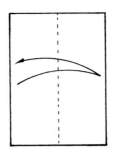

1. Fold a full size sheet of paper in half. Unfold.

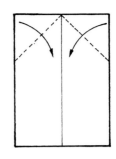

2. Fold down the top corners.

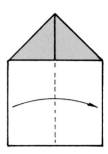

3. Fold in half.

4. Fold the top and bottom corners. Unfold.

5. Tuck in both corners.

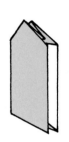

6. This will be the body of the Penguin.

MAKING THE WINGS

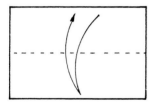

7. Fold a full-size sheet of paper in half. Unfold.

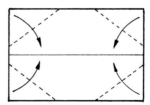

8. Fold the four corners to the center as shown. (See the next illustration.)

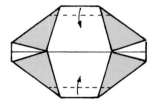

9. Fold the top and bottom edges.

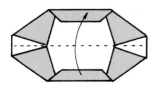

10. Fold in half.

11. Fold in half again.

12. Fold flaps on each side up as shown.

13. This will become the wings of the Penguin.

MAKING THE HEAD

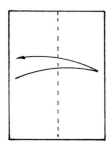

14. Fold a 1/2 sheet of paper in half. Unfold.

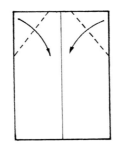

15. Fold down the top corners *nearly* to the center as shown.

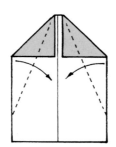

16. Fold both edges *nearly* to the center as shown.

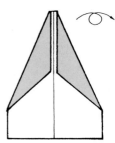

17. Turn over.

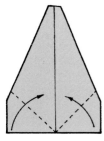

18. Fold the bottom corners up to the center.

19. Fold the bottom corner to the edge of the last fold.

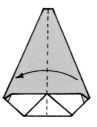

20. Fold in half.

21. Fold down the top triangle. Unfold.

22. Tuck in the top triangle.

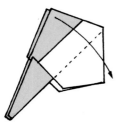

23. Fold down *only* the top layer.

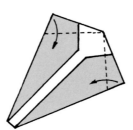

24. Fold both corners.

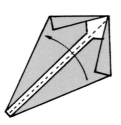

25. Fold the bottom half up.

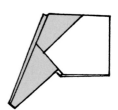

26. The head of the Penguin should look like this.

MAKING THE LEGS

27. With a 1/2 sheet of paper, make the BOOT shape. Fold the left bottom corner up. Unfold.

28. Tuck in the corner.

29. Fold each flap up to the side as shown.

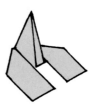

30. The legs of the Penguin should look like this.

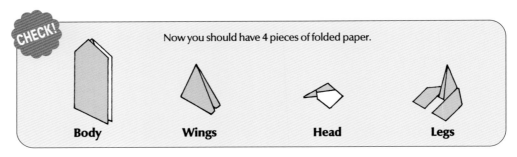

Now you should have 4 pieces of folded paper.

Body **Wings** **Head** **Legs**

● Let's put them together and make a Penguin. This will require glue or paste to hold the shapes in place. ●

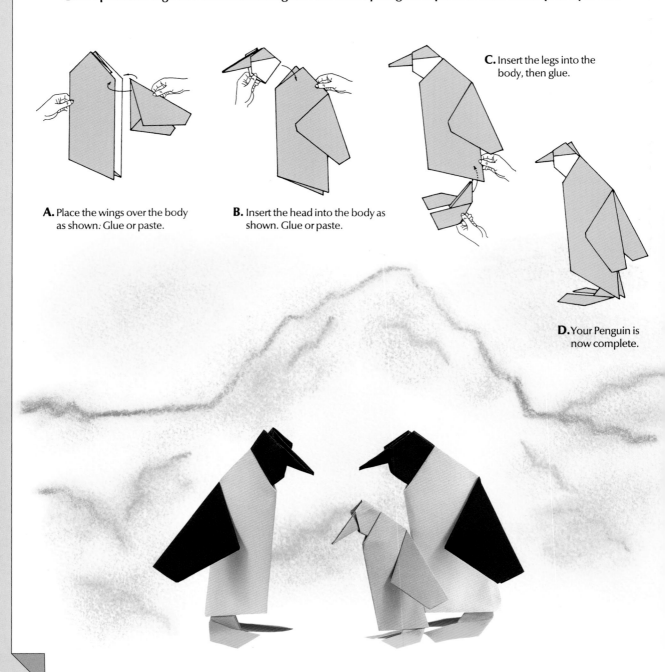

A. Place the wings over the body as shown: Glue or paste.

B. Insert the head into the body as shown. Glue or paste.

C. Insert the legs into the body, then glue.

D. Your Penguin is now complete.

EAGLE
level C

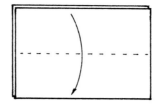

The eagle is a great hunter. He soars through the sky on powerful wings, searching for prey. You can open its wings and flap them. Many eagles have white necks. Try using white paper for the neck unit, brown for the body, and orange for the legs.

MATERIALS
5 sheets of rectangular-shaped paper
one 1/2 sheet of paper for the head and neck
one 1/4 sheet of paper for the beak

MAKING THE BODY

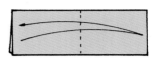

1. Fold two sheets of full-size paper in half.

2. Fold in half. Unfold.

3. Fold up the bottom corners of the top layer. Fold back the bottom corners of the reverse side. (NOTE: Follow the illustration carefully. The angles of the folds are different on the left and right sides.)

4. Fold the left corner down. Unfold.

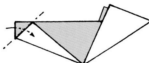

5. Tuck the left corner in.

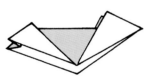

6. This will become the body of the Eagle.

MAKING THE HEAD & NECK

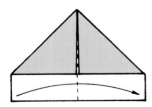

7. Fold a 1/2 sheet of paper to make the HOUSE shape. Fold in half.

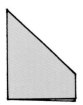

8. This will become the head and neck of the Eagle.

MAKING THE BEAK

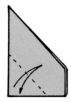

9. With a 1/4 sheet of paper, make the shape in step 8. Fold the left bottom corner up to the edge. Unfold.

10. Tuck in the corner. Rotate 90° counter-clockwise.

11. Fold the left side as shown. Unfold.

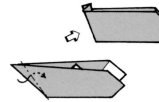

12. Tuck in the left side.

MAKING THE WINGS

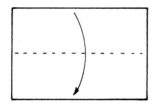

13. Fold a full-size sheet of paper in half horizontally.

14. Fold the left corner of the top layer up, then repeat for the bottom layer.

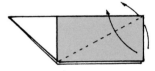

15. Fold the right corner up as shown. Repeat for the bottom layer.

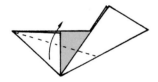

16. Fold the bottom corner of the top layer up.

17. This will become the *left wing*.

18. With another full-size sheet of paper, repeat steps 13 through 15, then fold the bottom corner of the *bottom layer* back as shown to complete the *right wing*.

MAKING THE LEGS

19. Use a full-size sheet of paper to make the BOOT shape. Fold the left bottom corner up. Unfold.

20. Tuck in the corner.

21. This will become the legs of the Eagle.

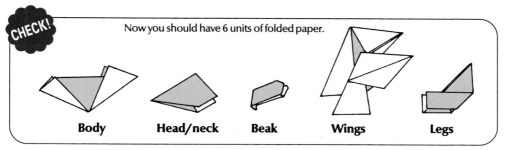

CHECK!

Now you should have 6 units of folded paper.

Body **Head/neck** **Beak** **Wings** **Legs**

● Let's put them together and make an Eagle. This will require glue or paste to hold the shapes in place. ●

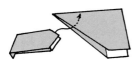

A. Insert the beak into the head/neck unit. Position it carefully, then glue or paste.

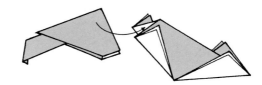

B. Insert the head assembly into the body as shown. Glue or paste in place.

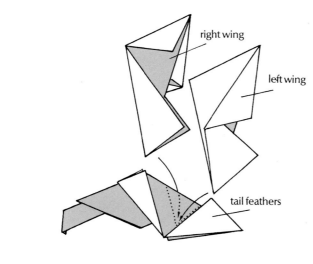

right wing

left wing

tail feathers

C. Place the left wing on the body, positioning it above the triangular tail feathers. Glue or paste in place. Do the same for the right wing.

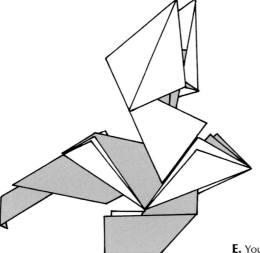

D. Insert the legs into the body as shown. Glue or paste in place. After glue has dried, spread the legs for stability if necessary.

E. Your Eagle is now complete.

MONKEY
level C

Monkeys walk on all four limbs or sit upright on their back legs. They love to eat fruit and play in the branches of trees in the tropical forest, which is their home. Since monkeys often travel in bands, make several so they can play together.

MATERIALS
4 sheets of rectangular-shaped paper

MAKING THE BACK LEGS

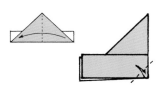

6. Make the BOOT shape. Fold up the right bottom corner. Unfold.

7. Tuck in the right corner. Fold up the left side corner up. Do the same for the reverse side.

8. This modified BOOT shape will be the back legs of the Monkey.

MAKING THE BODY & FRONT LEGS

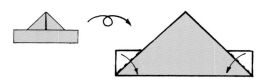

1. Make the MOUNTAIN shape. Fold both corners down.

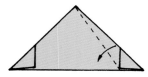

2. Fold the right edge as shown.

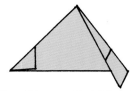

3. This will become the left front leg and body of the Monkey.

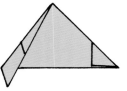

4. Make another MOUNTAIN shape and fold the *left* side in the same manner as step 2. This will become the *right* front leg and body.

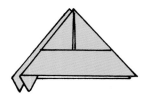

5. Join the two units and paste the center of the left edge only.

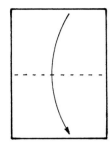

9. Fold a sheet of paper in half.

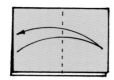

10. Fold in half again. Unfold.

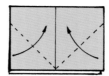

11. Fold up the bottom corners (top layer only).

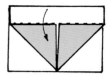

12. Fold down the top edge.

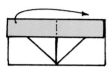

13. Fold back as shown.

14. The paper should look like this.

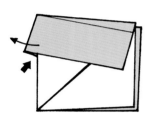

15. Pull the top rectangular section to the left as shown. The fold line of the top edge will shift. Fold the new line firmly. Rotate.

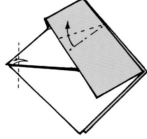

16. Fold as shown to make a tuck on the right flap. (This will become the cheek.) Repeat on the reverse side. Fold the left corner. Unfold.

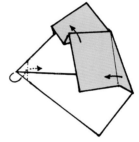

17. The ear flap should look like this. Shift the right edge as shown and make a new fold line. Fold firmly. Repeat on the reverse side. Tuck in the left corner.

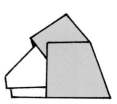

18. Tuck in the bottom flaps.

19. The head of the Monkey should look like this.

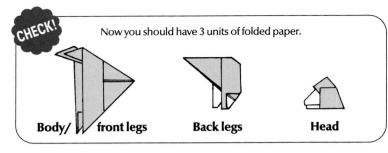

CHECK! Now you should have 3 units of folded paper.

Body/front legs   Back legs   Head

● Let's put them together and make a Monkey.
This will require glue or paste to hold the shapes in place. ●

The colored paper here makes 56 sheets of origami folding paper. Carefully separate a sheet of colored stock from the book, tearing gently along the perforated line. Then fold the paper in quarters and cut. This will give you 4 of the "full-sized sheets" used for all the animals in this book. See pages 4 and 5 for more details. ➙

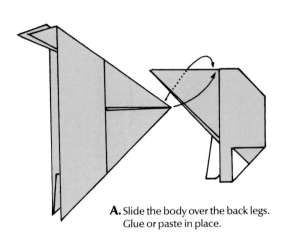

A. Slide the body over the back legs. Glue or paste in place.

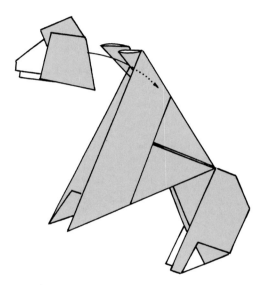

B. Insert the head between the small triangular flap of the body. Glue or paste in place.

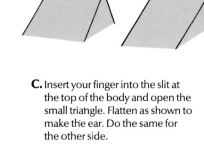

C. Insert your finger into the slit at the top of the body and open the small triangle. Flatten as shown to make the ear. Do the same for the other side.

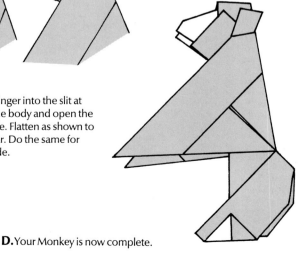

D. Your Monkey is now complete.